Global Human Trafficking In The Family Law

By: Randell D Stroud

2017

Table of Contents:

Forward and Introduction:

In the eyes of our father God, before the roots of mother nature, prior to any parent entering into a family law court-room, both father and mother are undoubtedly the full fledged guardians of any offspring they may have mutually created .Before a couple enters into the family law system, there is no one regulating the terms and conditions of parenthood, household income, time spent with the children, or any other related matters. However, as soon as you add a judge into the mix, lives can be forever altered by an ordinary human construct. The Family Law Courts!

On 3/8/2017, the United Nations Human Rights Council in Geneva, Switzerland, received a 30 page shadow report and an additional 31 pages of semi-classified US federal court documentation (to later be published after rulings are made) displaying the gross abuse of power within the family law courts; not only in the USA, but in nearly every country around the globe. This report was submitted by "yours truly".

The family law courts around the world have been responsible for mass incarceration of parents, widespread **Parental Alienation Syndrome** epidemics, abuse of children, racism towards Indigenous native populations, increased suicide risks, and other damaging consequences. Worst of all, this system that thrives off the famous slogan, "In the best interest of the children", is profiting from these abuses.

Gender discrimination against men and against mothers who wish to transfer custody to fathers without stigma, are under-documented problems we face in our ill social structure. Racism, rights of immigrants, women being sexually harassed in the work-place, failing economies; all of which are very important topics that deserve continued monitoring, yet the plight of children and parents, namely fathers, who get caught in the destructive nature of the modern domestic family law courts is deserving of equal consideration in terms of reformation or possible outright abolition of these regulations.

This report sheds light on the thousands of fathers, mothers, and children who have been negatively affected by the family law courts, with a specific focus on fathers. Since the popular phrase "Deadbeat Dad", became mainstream in the 1990's, society falsely believes that fathers who are not in their children's lives, always do so at their own discretion. Yes, some fathers do raise their children for a short period of time then abandon their children, despite cooperation from the mother; which is very disappointing; just as some mothers have also done. But, there are many other factors to consider when trying to understand why some men and women are deterred and what can be done to encourage their participation in the parenting process.

This report highlights the unique social challenges that men, women, children, and Indigenous populations face in the family law courts, as well as society as a whole.

Genital mutilation, forced military service, majority of homeless populations, majority of suicide cases, majority of bankruptcy filings, all attributed to men! In fact, there is a 2:1 odds in suicide cases showing that most men who commit suicide have either recently gone through a divorce/custody battle, or are in the process of doing so.

Since President Bill Clinton passed various federal mandates throughout his presidency increasing sanctions on unwed fathers and "accused" male spousal abusers, the incarceration rate of men has skyrocketed! Since 1994 to present, more than 70% of black children now grow up in single parent homes because their fathers are incarcerated or face economic hardship. The stats aren't much better for white fathers. In fact, studies show that children are more likely to grow up with a family pet than they are with their father! After divorces take place, men are likely to end up in poverty or in jail. In Massachusetts alone, fathers being arrested for getting behind on child support payments make up the bulk of the jail population. Before the 1990's, the rate of single parent homes in the black and white communities were significantly lower, especially in the lower income areas which often hit the black communities even harder, thus resulting in more incarcerations for the **Prison Industrial Complex.**

Ironically, Mr.Clinton himself has been dodging paternity test requests from his alleged illegitimate son, Danney Williams, since the 1990's. Perhaps the scorned Hillary decided to vicariously unleash her fury upon the entire male population through the executive powers of her husband. Alas, the issue isn't just with the USA. It is a global epidemic. In fact, recently, A fathers rights union filed suit against the government of Israel through the United Nations, whereas the International courts did condemn the "Tender years law" in Israel that disallows fathers to file for custody of their children until they reach the age of 7 with the arbitrary belief that, "Only mothers can care for children under the age of 7".

Another group that loses in family law courts are the Indigenous populations of the United States, who have very little sovereignty in cases of removal of indigenous children by DCS. (Department of Child Services.)

Please read my 31 page report with an open mind and come away with a new understanding of these issues. Nalini-Global is NOT a Women's rights organization, a Men's right organization, or a children's rights organization, but rather a HUMAN rights organization. Unbiased and clear, we discuss topics that the public may not be aware of. After reading this report, you will learn about the Prison Industrial complex, the Military Industrial complex, how the State is profiting from Mothers and Fathers, and most importantly, how the system is dividing the very essence of what it means to be a human being who is entitled to equal protection under the law.

I truly believe that this report will effectively blow the lid off of the family law court conspiracy. I believe that our current situation is caused by the "blowback" effect *(A popular CIA term used to describe the consequences of militaristic foreign policies)* .
 Marginalized groups of people are discriminated against or harmed, thus, those groups

seek more power, then that group becomes the discriminator, and the cycle of hate and war continues. Victims become bullies.

My report exposes the false presumption of "welfare spending is bankrupting countries", "Illegal immigrants have babies and don't pay taxes", "Men who cannot pay child support are deadbeat dads", "women who lose custody of their children are drugs addicts", ... all of these are stereotypes that are based on very loose understandings of a major social problem that is linked with bad economics and bad governance. --Namely, the criminalization of poverty.

My report is broad, generalized and covers many topics, it even dissects parts of the Federal Reserve system, yet, when you realize that the family unit is the starting point for any culture or nation of people, all of its other problems can be traced to it. The economy, war, military spending, crime,---it is all linked to the family law courts in some way.

We live in a time where we are supposed to pledge allegiance to flags and invisible borders, yet we must stay silent in our prayers to our chosen Gods, and we must ask for permission for nearly everything we do. Have you noticed that, in order to maintain your freedom, we are being exposed to an ever increasing number of laws and mandates in order to remain unincarcerated? 1 in 4 Americans will experience jail time in their lives. The United States of America has the largest prison population on Earth, with 75% of its inmates being incarcerated for NON-VIOLENT crimes (i.e. legal technicalities) it is a huge money making racket for the elites.

However, I am optimistic. With the publication of my report, among many other efforts and advocacy done on my part and by others, we can work together through the proper channels and get a conversation going! Creating more laws isn't the answer to creating a moral society. The more laws you create, the more criminals are inadvertently created. If wearing black socks became illegal, I would become a criminal in this very moment! It is truly that arbitrary. Simple words on paper, which can transform ordinary men and women into criminals who aren't allowed to drive a car, leave the country, or obtain employment. It is a cycle of destruction.

If you or someone who know has been effected by these issues, please read my report, print off as many copies as you can and send them to your legislators, governors, Prime Ministers, NGOS, Governmental bodies, or as a reference to your own research or case-work.

Many are chanting, "Let's make America great again"..... I say, **"Lets make humanity a family again."** That which affects men affects women, that which affects women effects men. We are interlinked in our struggles. It is high time we realize such truths.

Custody spats, Child support, alimony, these are all terms that send shivers down the spines of many. If you are a non-custodial parent or custodial parent, entering into the family law system, please consider these tips moving forward to ease the struggle of your unique family structure that is now being governed, not by the laws of nature, but by ordinary humans draped in robes combined with the backing of an oppressive fiat currency based economy. If you are reading this book, perhaps you are entering into the family law courts for the first time. Perhaps you have a friend of family member who is going for the first time. Perhaps you simply want to be prepared for it just in case it happens to you! After all, half of marriages end in divorce in the United States. Save the following tips for a "rainy day", I hope and pray that you will never have to test their efficacy.

Non-Custodial Parents:

1. **Get a DNA Test!** : This sounds like a no-brainer, but you'd be amazed at how many men are paying child support for a kid that is not biologically their own. Unless there is a prior adoption agreement, no one is legally obligated to pay for someone else's child.

2. **Consider communication:** If the child is yours, make one last effort to communicate with the mother. What are your goals with the child? What are her goals? Does she want to keep the child? Do you want to be a part of the child's life? Are you both financially sound? If you two can both find an agreement without involving the government, this will be your best bet. However, if any financial support is given to either party, keep receipts of everything. The custodial parent, (who is typically always going to be the mother in the eye's of the family law system), can bring the case before a judge at any time and thus sue you for retroactive support. Without any evidence of prior support, you could be on the hook for thousands of dollars.

3. **Consider your income:** When a child support case is brought to court for the first time, the court will ask for your previous year's tax return and proof of income from the last two months. If you know that you have a case coming up, it may be in your financial interest to research how your income levels will be considered. If you have been working three jobs for the last two months before your court date, the courts will consider that income for setting guidelines on how much you are to pay each month. While I do no advise anyone to do anything illegal, maneuvering within the rules (while still adhering to them), in order to survive the eventual 50% garnishment of your income that is soon to take place, is a worthy survival tactic.

4. **Never let an administrator set the guidelines for support!** The child support enforcement agency will often sell the idea to you that a judge is not needed. They will first appoint an administrator to have a meeting with you and the "custodial" parent. During this meeting, they will calculate income and expenses and then come up with an arbitrary number. That number will always favor the custodial parent. Never agree to their offers! Always demand that a judge make a ruling on the numbers. Remember, only the judge can make deviations from the state guidelines. The Child support enforcement administrators cannot make deviations; in fact, they are encouraged to calculate high numbers so that they can collect bonuses from the Title IV section D grant money that is linked with child support collections. However, if you demand to speak with a Judge, he/she may or may not, consider the fact if you have medical expenses, outrageous rent, or other

factors that impact your ability to earn income. If the judge is compassionate, you may get lucky with a ruling that is slightly lower than the recommended guidelines issued from the Child Support Enforcement Agency. However, the administrators will never tell you this because they know you are intimidated and do not wish to sit in a court room all day. While the administrators can quickly draw up an order and get you out of their offices, in the long-run, it may not benefit you.

5. **Be Careful with Modifications:** Just because you think your child support is too high doesn't mean a judge will agree. If you seek to modify your child support order, you may end up paying more! Especially if you earn more income than you did previously. In some states, CSE (child support enforcement) will automatically raise support amounts if the NCP (Non custodial parent) gets a higher paying job. It is a deadly cycle. Get a higher paying job to afford a child support order, only to have it raised again! Only seek modification if you experience a sharp decrease in earnings and/or you lose your job. Major medical expenses coming from a surgery or foreclosure may warrant a temporary reduction but can be risky. Consult an attorney!

6. **Challenge Expenses:** In child support cases, you will be made to pay for half of any day-care or medical costs. Be sure to challenge any receipts that appear home-made. These extra expenses can inflate child support payments very quickly, especially if the other parent is embellishing the amount they are paying for child-care costs.

7. **Ask for mediation:** Many courts will offer a no-cost, one-time, mediation session between you and the mother. This is your last ditch effort to sit privately in a room with you and the other parent to negotiate a parenting plan and/or to make voluntary reductions in support. While mediation can be extremely helpful if both parties are logical, it is still up to the judge to agree with the terms.

8. **Consider settlements or Forgiveness:** If you get behind in child support, you may be able to offer settlements to avoid jail time. If you owe $10,000 for instance, you may be able to offer the judge a $6,000 settlement to avoid jail-time without having to pay the remaining three. Some states even allow for forgiveness of child support debt if you have a good excuse such as medical problems and you are showing good faith to look for employment.

9. *Study Turner V Rogers*- This supreme court case outlined that non-custodial parents should only be jailed if they are **willfully** refusing to pay child-support payments. Being unable to pay does not warrant one's life or liberties to be suspended. It must be proven before such aggressive tactics can be implemented against the non-custodial parent.

10. *Study State of Minnesota V Nelson*- In this case, Mr. Nelson was behind over $80,000, on child support, however, he was still caring for and nurturing his children, i.e.- "Supporting", therefore the supreme court reversed his felony conviction of failure to pay child support.

11. **Study** *Coull vs. Rottman* - In this case, Mr.Coull was absolved of paying any child support due to Ms.Rottman alienating the child from Mr.Coull. The courts found that Ms.Rottman had no basis to ask for support if she was adamant on not

allowing the father to partake in the child's life despite him being fit to do so. This is a rare case decision, but very thought provoking.

12. **Consider International Law:** 1976 Article 11 of the ICCPR – International Covenant on Civil and Political Rights – came into effect stating, "No one shall be imprisoned merely on the ground of inability to fulfill a contractual obligation." This international obligation contradict many countries' domestic laws that allow for civil jailings. The United States being one of the chief offenders in not adhering to the provisions in this international agreement. Nevertheless, it is still noteworthy.

Custodial Parents:

1. **Communicate:** Do you want this child? Does he? Is abortion or adoption being considered? Can you sit down with him/her and have an open-dialogue about both of your futures? If the child has already been born, still communicate! Do everything you can to handle the situation without court involvement.

2. **Welfare-** Many states will not issue welfare to struggling parents unless they name both parents and/or agree to put one of the parents on child support. A good remedy is to have the entire family apply together, however, this often times makes one ineligible because your income bracket may be too high. Put your heads together and determine what would most benefit the family.

3. **Do not alienate your children:** If you are receiving child support, you are NOT a single parent doing it alone, you are getting help. Even if the other parent is not able to financially provide, if they are showing love to the child, you should not get in-between that bonding process, to do so can cause severe mental and emotional scars to the child that can make them more susceptible to deviant behavior as an adult not to mention the emotional damage done to the parent who is being prevented from seeing the child. No body wins in alienation. Children are not bargaining pieces..

4. **Spend wisely:** If you receive a good amount of child support every month, use what money is left over and put it in a trust fund for the child's future education. Many custodial parents like to use child support funds to spoil their children with toys or even themselves. In the long run, it does nothing for your children. It is called "child support", not an entertainment fund.

5. **Reconsider enforcing penalties:** Asking a judge to suspend the other parent's driver's license or to have him/her incarcerated only hurts you and the child. Such penalties will make it harder for him to find and keep employment, thus reducing the chances that you will ever see a dime in child support.

6. **Rethink "Support"-** Many custodial parents are extremely protective of their children, since they usually spend the most time with the child while the other parent is usually busy trying to keep up with child support or alimony payments. If you truly need "support", do not fight "joint custody". This way you have one parent taking responsibility half the time, and the other parent doing half the work. In many cases, child support may not even be warranted, in this case, everyone can win. If it isn't about the money, and you can check your emotions at the door, then joint custody shouldn't be an issue.

7. **Become an advocate-** About 92% of the time, women end up becoming the custodial parent. As a custodial parent, you have a lot of power. Don't abuse this power! Use it to advocate for equal parenting rights.

I am reminded of an old saying, "Those who desire to give away their power are the most powerful indeed." or as Confucius would say, "Those who wish to secure others, has already secured himself."

Both parties

Be mindful of eachother! Neither parent is in a particularly "easy" situation. While the non-custodial parent will become stressed out about meeting child-support criteria, the custodial parent will become stressed out with the rearing of the child, transporting the child ,ect. Try to put yourself in the other parent's shoes and practice empathy. If both parents can do this, it will make it easier for each of them to work together for the sake of the child and potentially remove the disagreements that lead to one of the parents allowing the government to regulate their family affairs.

While the media has given much coverage to the narrative of the "struggling single mom", whereas "Men need to step up or face the consequences", I believe that a new narrative needs to be introduced to the general public. One that considers the history of gender relations and how modern developments require us to look at the situation of family disputes through a modernized "looking glass".

This publication includes the un-redacted portions from a report that was submitted to the Human Rights Council in Geneva and to several other human rights organizations and/or governing bodies such as the United States Department of Justice. The original report was over 50 pages long, however, the sections shown in this publication exclude personal documents that are privileged to confidentiality. I pray that those who take the time to read this report will walk away with a better sense of how the modern family law system operates, who is being marginalized and what we can do to reduce its over-reach into our personal decisions. After all, true "freedom", isn't the just the ability to make a choice, but to also suffer the naturally occurring consequences of a choice-- absent of regulation.

"Freedom", teaches us that consequences rarely need to be administered by government, but rather by the laws of nature coming from karmic retributions, principles that no man-made legislation can create a loop-hole for. When economic profiteering is disguised as social justice, we have no choice but to unmask such wraiths, specters, and/or parasitic apparitions masquerading as defenders of the weak.

God-speed.

-Randell D. Stroud

Naliniglobal.wordpress.com

NALINI-GLOBAL

Global Human Trafficking in the Family Law Courts

By: Nalini-Global – 3/8/2017

R.D STROUD

Table of Contents:

I.   Introduction

My name is Randell Stroud, co-founder of Nalini-Global, an international human rights organization that studies the constitutionality of US domestic policies as well as foreign human rights abuses. I have certifications in International Law from Duke University, a Paralegal certification from Penn Foster Career College, experienced Chapter 7 Bankruptcy specialist, and I moonlight as a youth boxing coach. In this presentation, we will discuss gender inequality, its effects on the families/family law courts during custody disputes, how/who profits from such disputes, and what remedies can be proposed in order to solve the issues arising from them.

II.   Women's Rights, a struggle for acknowledgement: A culture study

Prior to the 1960's, traditionally, men have usually been classified as hunters, economic "bread-winners", warriors, and overall "leaders" of their families whereas women have been classified as "gatherers" and keepers of the home with the expectation to submit to their male-counterparts. During the rise of World War II, gender roles were shifted as men were drafted in the war leaving women to take on responsibilities usually reserved for men.

After WWII ended, men came home to find that their wives now had careers and a sense of independence that was once unheard of. Historically, women have had quite an uphill battle when it comes to pursuing individual careers and goals outside of becoming a homemaker. Women's suffrage, the recognition of work-place sexual harassment and the historic landmark ruling from *"ROE V WADE"*, which allowed women to seek out abortions legally, are among the three most prime examples that feminists cite in their struggle for equality, independence, and gender neutrality.

Speaking of work-place environments, to this day, "Gender pay-bias" *(the presumption that women with the same credentials as men are automatically paid lower salaries who assume the same job duties)*, is still a major concern among women's rights activists groups, that is not completely unfounded.

As a result of historical, world-wide and socially accepted domestic and sexual abuse of women, In 1979, *CEDAW (The Convention on the Elimination of all forms of Discrimination Against Women.)*, A United Nations sponsored international treaty, was implemented and has been ratified by 189 different states. Over 50 countries have ratified the treaty while others have simply become honorary "signers "of the treaty but have not ratified. Iran, Somalia, Sudan and Tonga have refused to even discuss the treaty. Surprisingly, the United States has not ratified the treaty, yet women enjoy relative freedom in terms of gender equality compared to most of the world.

During the 1995 case, *"People of State of California V O.J. Simpson"*, Mr. Simpson was accused of being abusive to and eventually murdering his then wife, Nicole Simpson. The evidence appeared strong against Mr. Simpson, yet he was able to secure a verdict of innocence. Silent victims of domestic violence began to publically speak out against the verdict causing a national dialogue regarding gender relations. As a result, the filing of restraining orders began surge in the late 1990's. In 2002, a bulletin from the U.S. office for Victims of Crime stated that "…in 1998 the national (restraining order)registry contained 97,136 entries", that same bulletin was re-released again in 2005 that stated .."there are more than 940,000 protection orders in our database" *(see acrosswalls.org/restraining-orders)*, whereas the majority of these cases were filed by women against former boyfriends or spouses.

In 1975, Congress created the Child Support Enforcement Agency in an attempt to reduce welfare expenditures, as a sort of "welfare recovery program". In the 1990's, President Bill Clinton passed a plethora of federal laws benefiting women including the "Personal Responsibility and Work Opportunity Act" and the "Deadbeat Parents Punishment Act of 1998", which increased punishments for non-custodial parents who got behind on child-support, including felony charges for non-custodial parents who live in a different state than the child in question. Revocation of passports, driver's licenses, garnishments of checks upwards to 60%, interception of income tax returns, and the requirement that non-custodial parents purchase health insurance for their children, all became the new norm.

(VAWA) or the **"Violence Against Women Act"** of 1994, was also passed during the Clinton administration. This bill gave the federal government the authority to award grant/restitution money to women claiming abuse for transitional housing and required HIV testing of not only those convicted of the attacks on women, but also of those simply charged/accused of the crime itself; A provision in the bill that was criticized by the *American Civil Liberties Union*. A women's rights activist, Janice Shaw-Course, from *the Concerned Women for America* group, attacked the bill stating, "The act ends up creating a climate where all men are viewed as violent and all women are viewed as victims. It creates a climate for false accusations." The legislation also opened up a path for citizenship for illegal aliens who claimed domestic abuse by an American citizen as a means of asylum, creating yet another incentive for false-allegations. The law has been amended in both 2005 and 2013 to include language that would not bar male victims of domestic violence from citing the same protections, thus far, no individual or organization has been able to successfully cite VAWA legislation in cases of female on male domestic violence cases.

In the last fifty years, we have seen the Marches Washington DC for both racial equality and women's rights activism. There is no question that both women and minorities have historically been marginalized in our society. However, many are now arguing that a reversal trend is now happening in terms of gender equality. In women's push for equality, portions of the movement have turned aggressively "anti-men". Instead of promoting "equality", a tone of "superiority" seems to have taken root. It's the classic, "bullied becomes bully" syndrome that has taken precedent in many feminists groups. In retaliation, "Men Rights" groups have begun to spring up, many of which mirror similar radical views that point to a deep-seeded disgust for women. Women burning their bras in public, walking down the street in the nude protesting what they call, "Rape-culture", whereas male rappers are uttering lines in their songs like, ***"Shoulda got a pre-nup"*** (pre-nuptial agreement)" , insinuating that most women are after men's financial assets. The gender war has reignited! The situation is similar to what CIA director "Michael Scheuer" described in his foreign policy assessments with a term known as "blowback". In military conflicts, an army will often preemptively strike a city or town known to harbor terrorists.

The attack is well intended, yet many innocent people end up being caught in the cross-fire who then begin to harbor hate in their hearts and eventually join terror groups themselves in order to seek vengeance. This is the essence of "blowback". A term that is very relevant in this conversation. The cycle of destruction has worked this way since the art of war-fare has been practiced in our human history. Unfortunately, some of those who pursue a political goal, display themselves in such a manner that discredits their efforts completely. While I have created a broad and general context for the upcoming sections in this proposal, it is clear that women in the United States and abroad have faced quite a few challenges and has produced many heroes as a result. To this day, child prostitution, genital mutilation, and other forms of abuse remain major problems here domestically and even more so in Northern Africa and Southeast Asia. Girls are usually the targets yet boys are increasingly becoming targets themselves.

Knowing all of this, no one can argue that women have endured abuse across the ages. However, is it possible that men too share societal burdens and marginalization that women do not? Regardless of who is discriminated against more frequently or harshly is irrelevant. As a human rights organization, any form of abuse or marginalization must be addressed. So if there is any marginalization or discrimination against the male gender, what examples and personal accounts can be shown?

III.   The challenges of manhood: Marginalized or farfetched?

We've all heard of *Roe V wade* , girls being abducted in human trafficking cases, and women winning their right to vote during suffrage. But, what struggles come with being a man?

The first thing that comes to my mind is the military draft! That's right! If you are born a male, chances are, you will be required to fight in a war if the government holding claim to your birth certificate asks you too. The classic term is called, "Conscription" or popularly known as "The Draft", a term made famous during the Vietnam War era draft, which was highly protested against during the 1960's anti-war movement. North Korea and Israel are quite famous for requiring military service of their female citizens, yet, In all but six countries that I know of, women are not called into mandatory service.

In the United States, administratively, "conscription" has been implemented through the "Selective Service Program". All males are required to sign up for the Selective Service Program(SSP) before the age of 18. Failure to do so can result in criminal prosecution, heavy fines, and being ineligible to receive any federal student loans.

The famous boxer, Muhammad Ali, is well-known for protesting his draft into the Vietnam War. In my own family alone, my uncle, a then aspiring minister, was also drafted into the Vietnam and refused to participate. The result for both Ali and my uncle was thousands of dollars in legal fees and years spent in court. Both men were successful in defending their refusal to be drafted, citing religious beliefs, but many other draftees were not as lucky. Some men were forced to flee to other countries, imprisoned, and in some cases, put to death; such as in the case of Eddie Slovik, who was put to death for refusing to fight in WWII. In the United States, punishments for those who refuse to participate in the SSP have began to transition more towards civil penalties over criminal penalties, yet the legality to do so remains.

In countries like Ethiopia, North Korea, Sudan, and many others, the threat of imprisonment and death still remain very likely for young men who refuse to be conscripted into military service. While women are required to be conscripted in fewer than ten countries around the world, the idea to conscribe women into the armed forces here in the United States has been recently discussed. In 2015, Sen.John McCain, stated that he would support legislation requiring women to sign up for the SSP , yet a bill was never implemented into law. Women's rights groups and mainstream news media pundits made statements such as, "Who will take care of the kids?", "Kids need their mother at home.", "Women aren't as physically strong to deal with service." , which begs the question, is it possible to play both sides of the fence when it comes to gender-studies and do fathers have an important place reserved in our hearts within human society?

"Ok, so men are conscribed into the military against their will, at least they aren't victims of genital mutilation (AKA-Female circumcisions in predominantly Muslim countries) ." Right? Wrong!

Boys in developed countries are more likely to experience genital mutilation than girls. Male circumcision is a wide-spread and unnecessary practice that takes place in 77% of births, according to the *Agency for Healthcare Research and Quality*. From a cultural standpoint, boys who don't undergo this procedure are often ridiculed and teased for the appearance of having uncircumcised genitalia. There have been countless studies on the so-called benefits of "male-circumcision", such as decreased risk of contracting Sexually Transmitted Diseases and lessening the difficulty in cleaning and maintaining proper hygiene of the male genitals. Conflicting studies of the degree of benefits from circumcision on both sides of the argument draw inconclusive results.

However, these "benefits", do not warrant involuntary surgery on a newborn babies (who lack the ability to consent) which are often done without anesthesia. The removing of foreskins, containing thousands of nerve endings, create a life-altering changes to a boy's body whereas the hospital itself that conducts the circumcision usually keeps the tissue to use in other procedures and studies, which creates a possible ethics issue. For the most part, the world, including western society, turns a blind-eye to such practices without second thought. To say that men are not without societal pressure is in an inaccurate statement.

Socially men are expected to have a chiseled physique, to be economic breadwinners, and to silently hold onto their pain in order to preserve their "masculinity". According to *AFSP.ORG*, "Men are 3.5 times more likely to commit suicide than women." When we look at divorce and custody verdicts, men are only about 7% likely to obtain full custody of their children and are almost always the ones left footing the bill which leads to increased risk of bankruptcy. As a former Bankruptcy Specialist employed by a major firm, I can confirm with first hand knowledge that nearly half of my clients filing for bankruptcy were men who were trying to keep up with child-support and alimony payments, the stress on their faces was evident. In fact, if you hear about a man committing suicide, 2:1 odds say that he was recently divorced or is in the process of going through a divorce. (*See Divorceinfo.com*)

Every year, thousands of men commit suicide after divorce, child support, and alimony orders are set into place. In many jurisdictions, alimony, unlike child support which typically stops at the age of 18, can be indefinite and carry the same repercussions for failure to pay child-support. (i.e- imprisonment, suspension of drivers license, garnishment up to 60% ect..)

The arguments that are for and against the constitutionality of required child support payments are numerous. Wherever you stand, it is clear that those who are required to pay child support and alimony are at an increased risk of filing bankruptcy, and anyone who is at risk for filing bankruptcy is most likely at risk for experiencing homelessness. The US interagency Council on Homelessness estimates that of the chronically homeless, 75% are male, 1 in 9 homeless people will eventually commit suicide. Let us take a look at some well known examples of how family law courts have affected men:

Derrick Miller, age 43, who found himself in the cycle of being unable to pay alimony/child-support, go to jail, lose job, cannot afford rent, get evicted, lose job, cannot pay alimony/child-support, go to jail...(rinse and repeat), took his own life on the stairs of a San Diego court house. He approached court officers stating, "You did this to me", before ending his life.

Randy Orville, age 33, of Illinois, hung himself on July 21,2003. Prior to his death, he was given a felony charge and was listed with 32 parents as being "Most Wants Deadbeat Parents" in the area. The courts believed that Mr. Orville would rather have his license revoked, have his property seized, lose his voting rights, and sit in a jail cell than to pay child-support. But, what sane person would purposely want that? Mr. Orville simply couldn't keep up with the crime of being a low-income father.

Trevor Goddard, 37, North Hollywood, committed suicide on June 8th, 2003 who had worked on films like Mortal Kombat, Men of War, JAG.... Killed himself in the midst of a messy divorce/custody battle.

David Guin, 38, incarnated for being behind on child support payments, hung himself on November, 1998.

Former NFL player, Robert Meachem, jailed for un-paid child support. He was ordered to pay 20K per month in child support, almost more than some people make in a year.

Navy Veteran and activist, Kash Jackson, has $900 of his $1600 retirement check garnished each month for child support. Jackson is also ordered to pay a fluctuating amount of approximately $2,000 per month for his two sons. The reason why it fluctuates is that Jackson was told he had to reimburse his ex-wife, who makes over $85,000 per year, for whatever childcare and extra-curricular activities that she claims. After garnishments, Jackson is left with only $700 per month to pay rent and feed himself. Recently Mr.Jackson was sentenced to 30 days in jail for falling behind in payments. His debt will continue to accumulate while incarcerated.

Dimitrius Underwood, age 22, defensive end for the Miami Dolphins, slit his own throat when police issued a warrant for his arrest for felony charges of missed child support payments.

Speaking of lives ruined by unnecessary litigation, another plight that men must face are "false allegations of rape". According to FBI reports from 1996, statistics have consistently put the number of "unfounded" rape accusations around 8%, while some studies say it's closer to 10%. However, the actual percentage is extremely difficult to pin-point. The 8% of cases that were determined to be "false-accusations", could have in-fact been legitimate, whereas in the cases were convictions were obtained, they could have been false. The numbers being presented to the public could be higher or lower. The reason why true rape conviction statistics are highly debated is because of the **discretion** exercised by judges in such cases. Let us present a scenario.

1. John and Sally have sex at 4:00pm. Later that evening, Sally has second thoughts about what happened and decides to report the act as rape. Investigators find traces of semen on the leg of Sally that match the DNA of John's. Sally cries in court claiming, "I did not consent". John shouts, "She didn't resist at all. She wanted it. It was consensual." Did John rape Sally? Your guess is as good as mine!

What makes these cases even harder to determine is the fact that not all rape cases involve evidence of physical attack. Many of us imagine a rape as a man who attacks a woman physically (punching and kicking her) and forces his way onto her. However, as many legitimate rape victims have testified, rapists have used methods of "date-rape" drugs, verbal threats, intimidation through use of firearms and other weapons, things that wouldn't leave behind any physical evidence of bodily harm. All the more reason why sexual education teachers should not only warn students about STDs and unwanted pregnancy, but also the importance of developing **emotional trust** with a potential sexual partner. Some California Universities have even gone so far as requiring their students to carry "Sexual Consent Contract Forms" whereas the couples must take a picture of themselves signing the contract before the act takes place. How sad that our young boys and girls have to grow up in such a volatile dating environment!

A good example is the famous case of Brian Banks, former Atlanta Falcons lineman, who was arrested and charged with raping classmate, Wanetta Gibson, in 2002. He was facing 41 years to life in prison and ended up accepting a 5 year plea deal for a case that looked appeared unwinnable.

Gibson was awarded $1.5 million in civil court, who sued the local school district claiming that school employees failed to guarantee a safe environment for her. In 2011, Banks messaged Gibson through *Facebook*, who agreed to meet up and discuss the accusations. During the meeting, Banks had a hidden tape recorder in his pocket which captured Gibson boasting about her false-accusations. With help from *California Innocence Project* and Los Angeles county prosecutors, Bank's rape conviction was officially overturned after spending five years in prison for a crime her never committed. Gibson was later counter-sued by the school district to recover the funds she had previously sued them for, plus punitive damages.

Banks now serves as a spokesperson for the *California Innocence Project* and is working on a documentary about his story.

The worst part about this story is that it devalues the plight of **true** rape victims. The crime of rape is one of the worst actions a human can take against another. However, when the standard of culpability is so ambiguous in such cases, emotions can run high and weigh heavily upon a juror, which does present risks for false-convictions. Biologically, a male must "penetrate" a female in order for intercourse to occur, thus, males always appear to be the instigators and initiators of sexual activities. Logically speaking, this is why female on male rape cases are almost unheard of. While not impossible, the impracticality of it makes it a rare occurrence. Nevertheless, engaging in casual sex runs a very high risk of STDs, pregnancy, and false accusations of rape occurring on part of males, and actual rapes occurring on part of females. (Subject material that is rarely discussed in sexual education.) Topics that should be addressed to teens and young adults in today's litigious society.

The price, or should I say, the "risks" of being a man, a divorced man, or an unwed father is quite high in western society. If it weren't a crime to be a man, then fathers/husbands would not hold the title of "defendant" in family law courts, nor would Human Services take "mugshots" of alleged fathers during paternity testing. Is it really moral that a person, primarily women, can divorce a man and receive financial rewards for the remainder of their lives in the form of indefinite alimony? What are the advantages of a man wanting marriage/children in the 21st century? What has society made of the husband and of the father? How can we bring back the era of Kings and Queens? The true nature of male/female relationships according to our creator. Let us dig deeper.

IV.   Human Trafficking & Ramifications of Family law Courts on Families

Take it from me, a man who has participated in the family and domestic courts both as a child and as an adult. My own father has gone through that same system twice as an adult. My half-sister, a child he bore with a short-term girlfriend before meeting my mother, was alienated from my family. The mother vigorously sought after my father's income and resisted him in visitation matters. I did not meet her until I was 13 and haven't seen her since. A trend that is far too familiar in the family law courts. At the age of 14, my parents divorced, whereas I did not re-establish a relationship with my father until my mid 20's. In both situations, my father was demonized as being "weak" and "uncaring", something I later learned that was quite untrue. This system is turning fathers into scared fugitives who are not necessarily "Deadbeats" but "Dead-broke" and "Dead-Tired".

7

According to *"DivorceMag.com"* , (sic).."*Nearly every major study produced on father-child relationships, show that fathers lose contact with their children within two years after a divorce. The percentage increases if the father has a low-income.*"

Title 18 subsection 1201 & 1202, strictly prohibits ransom, trafficking and kidnapping of children. Alas, if it done so under the arbitrary discretion of a state department, then a sort of "philosophical" immunity is granted upon themselves so it would seem.

In the last section, I was dissecting the child support system and how it can negatively effect "non-custodial parents" (who are typically men.) Let me take you through a personal scenario regarding my own son.

I was once attending an administrative hearing to discuss child support modification and how amounts are calculated. The judge, who is a paid employee of the state, the witness (A Tennessee Human Services employee- Also paid by the state), and the state's attorney (also paid by the state) acting on behalf of the petitioner (aka the custodial parent-mother) were all present to conspire against me. The judge asked if I had any questions for the human services employee. I asked, "where does my child support payments go." The woman from human services replied, "To the mother." I followed up by saying, "Does the state of Tennessee profit in any way, shape or form from these child support payments?" The judge stood up and said, "She doesn't have to answer that. If you can't afford payments, consider getting a second job." To be frank, child support is simply a "welfare recovery program." The federal government, by law, does not allow funding to any state without that state having a child support enforcement agency in full function. In fact, when applying for TANF or Non-TANF welfare benefits where children are involved, the state will usually refuse benefits to filers who cannot provide the names of both parents or limit assistance.

Oftentimes custodial parents will receive child support checks from the state in amounts as low as $1.The reason? Because the agencies are keeping portions of child support payments to recover welfare payments previously paid out to the custodial parent, thus giving the illusion that the non-custodial parent is not making an effort. Some may say, "Why should the government take on financial responsibility for a child?" The same argument can be made for the TARP program (Troubled Asset Relief Program) implemented by President Bush and continued by President Obama. A program that gave out over $475 billion dollars, tax-free, to failing corporations in order to address the mortgage and auto-industry crisis.

Where did this money come from? Thanks to the Federal Reserve Act of 1913, the Federal government can operate on what is called "Quantitative Easing", a process that allows the Federal Reserve to arbitrarily print out and loan out unlimited amounts of Federal Reserve notes (AKA-Dollars) to the Federal government. Worries of hyper-inflation, and financial bubbles have been repeatedly addressed by Federal Reserve critics such as Congressman Ron Paul, who has frequently called for a full audit and dismantling of the Federal Reserve on countless occasions with minimal support from congress. *Forbes Magazine* released an article in 2014 showing that *Boeing* alone received $13 billion in government handouts. Over 37.5 billion dollars in subsidies were given to big oil tycoon according to alternative media source *(US UNCUT)* . Just a year prior, The Tax Foundation released a study showing that special tax provisions for corporations saved them over $100 billion dollars, yet the middle class is stuck footing the bill and financial obligations of the income tax provisions in the U.S. Tax code.

Many Americans falsely believe that the income tax is how the federal government is funded and operated. This is simply not true. During Ronald Reagan's tenure, he instituted the "Grace Commission", a task force that was designed to uncover exactly how money collected from federal income taxes were being spent. The task force uncovered that less than 1% of the money went towards social programs and infrastructure, the remainder of it went towards overseas military spending, and to pay off the **interest** on the national debt, which hovers well over 16 trillion dollars today according to mainstream media sources, a figure that 5th District Congressman, Jim Cooper, of Nashville, Tennessee, disputes. Cooper says, *"Congress doesn't even know what the real numbers are, the real national debt isn't $16 trillion. I wish it were that low. The real national debt is closer to $60 or $80 trillion."*. So, to say that the federal government has to enforce child support orders because welfare payments are causing a deficit is laughable.

Currently, the United States of America has approximately 900 military bases in over 130 countries, whereas the average military expenditures per year hasn't dropped below $500 billion since 2003. The military budget in 2015 was over $600 billion. *(Source, Council on Foreign Relations, Business Insider Magazine)*

According to CNN, the US government gave over $35 billion dollars to foreign governments for aid. That is money that could have been used to help struggling mothers, fathers, and children here in the homeland. The worst part is all of this free money that is being handed over to corporations and foreign governments are given without threats of imprisonment if it is not paid back, in fact, they are not even asked to pay it back, it is a gift. So how does this all relate to child support/alimony payments? How do most state governments calculate what a "non-custodial parent-Father" should owe to the mother/child?

Each state has a different formula for calculating child support. Some states use a flat percentage, while most have adopted an arbitrary algorithm model that looks at both parent's incomes. On the surface, it seems fair until the custodial parent lists down things like, child-care and after school costs.

In many cases, these numbers are guesstimates given by the custodial parent. In the state of Tennessee, if both parents gross 25K per year for a 2 year old child, the father will most likely be paying about $500 per month. Then the mother may say, "But, I am paying $150 per week in day care costs to my neighbor." (which the father will be mandated to pay half of, then the state, by law, will force the father to pay for the health-insurance for the child which brings his monthly obligation closer to $700 per month (If alimony is factored in, double that amount!). The father then recommends that his grandmother watches the child to reduce child-care costs, but the court will inform him that the non-custodial parent has no "right" to make that choice. Let's dig a bit deeper in this "what if" scenario.

The child is already 2 years old, the mother filed 6 months ago, the father just recently learned of the child's existence, so now the court demands that he pay child support for the months he wasn't aware of the child. His debt would now be close to $6,000-$10,000, which puts him in instant arrears, causing him to lose his passport, essentially making him a prisoner in his own country. Even though the Universal Declaration of Human Rights explicitly recognizes the right of a person to travel freely and choose his nationality. *(See Article 13 of the UDHR).,*

(If any welfare benefits were paid to the mother, the father is also expected to pay the government back.)

The courts will tell the father that the $6,000 or so dollars is considered "retroactive" or "back-support", not **criminal arrears**. Yet the fact that his passport is instantly revoked shows us that the courts expect the father to leave the country as if he were a convicted criminal or fugitive. In fact, during any divorce or child support/custody proceeding, the mother will be called "The petitioner", "The mother", "The Custodial parent", whereas the father will typically be called "The Defendant", a title that is usually reserved for someone who is accused of a crime. The implication that you are a criminal and not a father, is evident from the onset of these cases. The entire proceeding is a feminist paradise. Even the child support collection offices are typically and disproportionately staffed with women.

Laws like *"Title IX"* of the federal code, which require a certain amount of women to be present in educational and sporting programs or the idea of "Affirmative action", does not seem to be present in the case of lack of male employees in the family law/child services sectors.

After child support, taxes, alimony, Medicare, and other deductions, suddenly, a father who was once earning 25k per year(Gross), is now taking home just a fraction of that, with no second thoughts from the courts of how he will eat or maintain a shelter for himself. Whereas if the mother has any difficulty, the state is ready to step in to assist her with housing, education, or any other needs.

After a typical child support case is heard, (which always comes first before custody is discussed; further evidence that monetary policies supersede parent/child boding), the judge will notify you that you are now responsible for all court costs and you must pay for the legal fees of the mother who just hired an attorney for $10,000 to take you to the cleaners. Failure to pay the fees will result in a license suspension.

The judge will then state that if you disagree with the child support amount set, you can file for a "Motion of Modification" in order to lower the amount or to suspend payments if you are fired from your job or your income is reduced. (A process that can sometimes takes months to accomplish; if accomplished at all.) Conversely, the Department of Human Services will track the father's employment history by his Social Security Number, whereas the mother will be notified anytime the father changes jobs and/or if he is earning more, thus encouraging the mother to file for modification to raise the amount on the child support order. Fathers are given child support orders they cant afford, so they seek higher paying jobs only to learn that their higher paying job results in higher child support payments, thus negating any benefit to his own living standard. Since Child support amounts do not have a "cap", essentially, a wealthy man making $100,000 per month, would have to potentially pay the mother upwards to $60,000 per month in child support, an amount that far exceeds what any child would need to live comfortably. It is safe to say that the mother will be pocketing 98% of that money obtained.

After child support is discussed, the judge will then bring up the topic of custody. The father will say, "I want 50/50 custody." If the father is lucky, the custodial parent will be agreeable, but if she were agreeable, you wouldn't be in court! The mother, as a revenge tactic, is likely to state, "He is dangerous, I'll allow him to **supervised** visitation only."-It is a glorified way of saying that, you can spend time with your child four days a month while a government agent follows you around taking notes, as if you were convict in prison.- Because domestic courts are considered, "discretionary" courts, the judge does not have to rule solely on evidence but rather on his own determinations, which is usually a determination that will necessitate the lawyers and the courts to be more involved and needed. If the courts aren't needed, then their justification for employment and increased funding for department budgets will not remain valid!

9 times out of 10, the judge will grant supervised visitation, but there is no guarantee that the mother will even comply with that order. If the father wants more than this, he will have to come up with his own funding for a lawyer since the court will not provide one for him like they would the mother. The father will also not qualify for any major public assistance, section 8 housing, or free educational programs, since he is making too much money from working 80 hours a week to keep up with child support/alimony payments.

If the father consistently displays "good behavior" during supervised visitations for at least six months without any negative or false allegations from the mother, the judge will then typically grant "general visitation", (4 days a month without supervision: because you are not a parent, but a "visitor"). If the mother does not cooperate with the order, you can file an injunction complaint with the court, where the mother will deny your allegations. At this point, you may decide to hire a lawyer in order to fight for 50/50 or even full custody. (Whereas you have a 7% chance of winning according to every major study).

6 months later, you find yourself in debt from legal fees, fighting for the right to be in your child's life which makes child support/alimony payments impossible to keep up with. Then the mother requests that you are to have your license revoked, making it difficult to find/keep a decent paying job which leads to arrests, homelessness, depression, alcohol abuse, and increased risk for suicidal thoughts. You can see the cycle that is to come. Debt, prison, and eventually a broken father who no longer cares. He will be labeled a "deadbeat" father by the society at large.

Some custodial parents will even go so far as to file bogus restraining orders on the non-custodial parent. Similar to Family law courts, domestic courts that preside over restraining order dockets are also considered "discretionary" courts, meaning that judges can ignore lack of evidence and rule in favor of a petitioner based on his "gut feeling". From my experience and research, restraining order dockets usually consists of women filing against men. (boyfriends, husbands, ect..). I have set in on dozens of such dockets, and nearly 99% of the cases were granted in favor of the female petitioner.

A few tears and a half-way convincing story with very little if any discovery, most judges will grant a restraining order 9 out of 10 times. They are very tough cases to beat. As a result, the person who loses the restraining order case will be barred from seeing his children for up to a full year, will have his 2nd amendment right to bear arms suspended, the order will be on his record effecting his ability to gain employment, and he will be burdened with paying all of the court costs including any lawyer fees that the petitioner may have racked up. If he is too poor to pay the court costs, he could have his license revoked. It is unbelievably easy to put a restraining order on someone and ruin their lives. The courts are ok with it because of its quick process and profitability in positive judgments. When you consider that the losing party must pay $200 in court costs per case and there are 50 cases on the docket, just do the math!

By some miracle, if the "FATHER" (non-custodial parent AKA Defendant), is lucky enough to gain 50/50 custody, he will still most likely be held liable for some child support payments.

If the father cannot keep up with payments, he is labeled a "dead-beat father", if he doesn't spend time with his children because he works 80 hours a week, he will still be called a deadbeat for lack of involvement. If by the grace of god, the father wins FULL CUSTODY, men typically do not ask the mother for child support or simply do not enforce orders against the mother like the mother would against the father.

21

As mentioned several times earlier, men are only about 7% likely to obtain full custody of their children. According to a report from the U.S Census Bureau, custodial fathers were owed $3.7 billion dollars in child support in 2011, while custodial mothers were owed around 31.7 billion. While the numbers for custodial mothers are much higher, we must take into consideration that only 7% of fathers are "entitled" to collect child support from mothers. According to an article posted by Dr. Helen Smith taken from the organization, "Fathers and Families", between 95% and 98.5 of all inmates in Massachusetts were males charged from probate and family law courts. Speaking simply, most custodial fathers do not seek arrest warrants against non-custodial mothers who are in arrears.

...Based on national data, if incarceration for non-payment of child support occurred at equal rates for men and women for arrearage of child support payments, 88% would be men, not the current 98.5%, women are incarcerated at a rate eight times less than men. " – From Fathers and Families Organization

Many poverty stricken fathers resort to working cash jobs, fudging their tax returns, or in extreme cases, leaving their host country in order to avoid the "debtor's prisons" caused by child support and alimony sanctions. The Office of Child Support Enforcement now hunts down fathers in more than 30 different countries who have signed international treaties with the United States created during the "Hague Convention" in November of 2007. In days of past, many American men would flee to France to join the French-Legion, a French quasi-military force that accepts foreigners, in order to escape lifetime alimony payments. These actions are now being targeted by the international community.

Many will make the argument that a man should financially contribute to the upbringing of his children. I don't think many would disagree under most circumstances. However, there are many inconsistent fallacies in our modern family law system. Let us paint a scenario.

1. A married man and woman have a child together. : Married woman works. Married man is unemployed. Both live together. Man does not contribute to household. The man is lazy and only watches TV. No criminal or civil sanctions are put on the man. There is no law stating that the man must work or contribute to the household because he is married.

2. Woman divorces man: The woman automatically gets default custody. The man is now liable for child support, her legal fees and has to fight for custody rights.

3. Woman receives child support payments from man; woman quits job; Man must pay more child-support to compensate for her lack of employment.

Essentially, it is illegal for a man in the United States, and most other countries, to get a woman pregnant out of wedlock. A married man can be as lazy as he wants legally without repercussion, but the moment he gets a divorce, he becomes a criminal. The courts will even label him as a **defendant**.

Why on Earth does a mother get default custody of a child? Why must a man "prove" his ability to be a father in court while spending thousands in order to get basic "visiting" rights? (80 days per calendar year, with over 4,000 days missed over the course of a child's life). I visit the park, I visit the shopping mall, I visit inmates in jail, but a parent should never have to "visit" his/her minor child.

The Huffington Post released an article on 5/30/2013 titled, *"How much does the average Divorce really Cost?"* The ballpark was between 5k-15k dollars for the average American. Could you imagine having to pay those kinds of lawyer fees while fighting keep up with child support payments while fighting to ibtain the basic the right to see your child? A process that could cost you up to $30,000 or more in legal fees.

Speaking of child support payments, who is paying them and who isn't?

"There are a lot of men who pay child support without issue. Not every man who is ordered to pay child support has a horror story behind him."

These are the words spoken by those who are truly uninformed and inexperienced in the family law human trafficking practice.

A study from the Urban Institute that took place between 2003-2004, showed that, men who make $42,000 per year (the national medium income) or above, typically had fewer issues keeping up with child support payments, whereas anyone who made under that amount was considered "high risk" for going into arrears. If this is known, then why aren't public institutions seeking a solution to help fathers?

Let us not single out women leaders who are also speaking up for fathers. Jacquelyn Boggess, from the *Center for Family Policy and Practice*, told NPR, "(The child support system) we're asking that women and children become dependent on men who are just as poor as they are."...... "Instead of motivating men to obtain higher paying jobs, the system is scaring them away, forcing them underground."

She went on to say, ... "We found 20 and 30 year old children that are paying their father's child support arrearages so that they can keep whatever little income they may have." The worst part is if men are arrested for any reason, child support does not automatically get suspended, they are expected to file motions to suspend their child support payments while incarcerated! If they fail to get the proper legal help while incarcerated, the debt continues to grow at an interest rate of 12% APR!

The Department of Human Services has advocates for mothers and children who offer legal assistance, housing assistance, educational assistance, and so forth, yet fathers are told to hire their own attorneys and to get a second job if they have financial hardship. Ignoring the 6th amendment, the courts have upheld that fathers are not entitled to public defender services in family-law court. Legal fees are just another factor that contributes to homelessness for non-custodial fathers. According to *"The Housing Spotlight-Who lives in Federally Assisted Housing? 2012"*, it was found that over 83% of voucher-holding applicants for housing were women. Single fathers who earn an income, despite having to pay out alimony and child-support usually don't qualify. The Department of Human Services has an entire program staffed with case workers to assist custodial-mothers, yet fathers are treated as criminal debtors. There is absolutely no sympathy for them in the courts. There is just too much money being made by the courts and the custodial parents. Debtor's prisons have been essentially unheard for nearly 200 years in the United States, yet the similarities between family law courts and debtor's prisons are astounding. But there is another enemy in this equation. The highly profitable **Prison Industrial Complex.**

In my previous shadow report, *"Civil Asset Forfeiture in California" (Naliniglobal.wordpress.com)*, I outlined the practice of private prisons partnering with public governments who profit from mass-incarceration and civil asset forfeiture (illegally seizing property then selling it for government gain). The practice is known as "policing for profit".

13

Private prisons make about $22,000 per inmate per year according to the Department of Justice. Lawyers are making between $5-15k per divorce, Custodial mothers are collecting alimony and child-support, and law enforcement is taking in over 5 billion dollars per year from civil asset forfeiture practices, whereas burglaries only result in about 4 million dollars worth of damage per year. In 2014 alone, law enforcement seized and sold more property than what burglars stole! *(See Martin Armstrong's article from "Armstrong Economics"- civil asset forefeiture supported by the Institute of Justice.)*

There is just too much power and incentive to NOT change the system as it is. The lack of respect that the role of "father" has in the western world is shocking and horrifying. Does the world have a love affair with mothers? Are mothers more influential to a child's development than a father's? According to the retail analysts at *"Repricer-Express"*, in nearly every country around the world, people spend twice as much on Mother's Day than they do on Father's day, with the exception being France, who is closer to an even amount.. Whereas 63% of 1500 CEOs and human resource directors were polled saying "It is not reasonable to give new fathers paid paternity leave." *(J.H. Pleck, "Family Supportive Employer Policies", Center for research in women)*

This is a somewhat comical and arbitrary observation. However, the real question remains, do fathers matter and what impact do they make on children? Or a better question is, what effects does an absentee father have on children, in particular, boys?

According to Edward Kruk, Ph.d. studies in , "The Vital Importance of Paternal Presence in Children's Lives." May 23, 2012 , - **71% of high school dropouts have absentee fathers in their lives.**

The US Census Bureau states that 23.6% of US Children lived in homes without a full-time father circa 2014. This means that children are more likely to grow up with a family pet than they are their own fathers.

Fatherhoodfactor.com, Contains a plethora of citations and research results that links increased suicide rates, higher chances of living in poverty, risks of being sexually abused, and just about every other social ill, all linked to fatherless homes.

One statistic particularly caught my eye. According to *Marushak, L.M. (2010).Parents in Prison and their minor children. Washington D.C, Bureau of Justice and Statistics,* children with an incarcerated father grew 79% from 1991 to 2007, about the same time that President Clinton began to enact penalties against those who would not or could not pay child support.

In, *A.Anne Hill and June O'Neil's, "Underclass Behaviors in the United States", CUNY, Baruch College, 1993*, their studies concluded that boys who grew up without fathers were almost three times more likely to engage in criminal activities that lead to incarceration than the mere 13% of inmates who come from homes where fathers were present.

A deadly cycle indeed! A father goes to jail for unpaid child-support, gets lost in the system, is driven underground or worse to suicidal tendencies, then his son is statistically set on a repeat course for himself. When it costs the state approximately $20,000 per year to feed, cloth, and house an inmate, you would think that it would be in the government's best interest and in the child's best interest to not only support the idea of a strong mother but strong fathers also. I suppose the current paradigm is far too profitable for their federally funded departments which outweigh the need to develop fatherhood participation.

By encouraging and investing in our would-be fathers, the bulk of society's problems could be greatly reduced. In the 1950's, when divorce rates were half of what they are today (approximately 50% of higher), crime rates were drastically lower.

The Federal Laws and increased sanctions enacted against American "non-custodial" fathers in the 1990's by President Bill Clinton, did not encourage fathers to participate in their children's lives, but discouraged it. In an ironic turn of events, Danney Williams, who claims to be Bill Clinton's illegitimate son, has repeatedly requested since the mid 1990's, that Mr. Clinton submit to DNA testing in order to establish paternity. To this day, Mr. Clinton denies the claim and has refused to participate in any court proceedings according to the testimony of Mr. Williams. Who could blame him? If paternity is established, Mr. Clinton could hypothetically be on the hook for major civil and criminal liabilities. Perhaps all of those harsh executive orders he enacted against the male population were stemmed out of his own guilt or instructions from a scorned Mrs. Clinton? Maybe we will never know. Either way, the legal consequences of such allegations are no laughing matter, especially under the laws he helped enact.

When you threaten someone with sanctions and penalties, it does not excite participation or increase motivation but rather it encourages one to flee. It harbors resentments towards children who had no say in whether or not they were to be born. It turns children into commodities, victims of human trafficking, and weapons of war, and how can any man love or be excited around a weapon? How awful is it that a human life can be turned into a legal instrument of liability? It doesn't surprise me that many fathers turn and run; because they are overwhelmed and frightened for similar reasons women seek abortions. The entire process can be daunting and draining, especially for a system who provides no encouragement or "Fatherhood Development Programs."

Alas, this should not surprise us. Since when did fathers ever have a choice to begin with anyways? Which brings us into a perfect segue for our next topic. "The choice of parenthood." Who has it and who doesn't?

Off the top of my head, there are more than 20 different ways for a woman to prevent parenthood, many of which are federally funded. IUD's, Birth Control Pills, Cervical Caps, Birth Control Shots, Plan B, Fallopian Tube surgery, ect... Men basically have Condoms and/or Vasectomies at their disposal.

Post-Pregnancy, women can opt to abort (or murder, depending on your viewpoint), the growing life-form in the body, or thanks to the "Safe Haven Laws" first Passed In Texas, a mother can legally drop off an unwanted child at a police department or firehouse. In the family law codebook, custodial parents have page after page stating their "rights", whereas non-custodial parents have about two paragraphs.

The best privilege that women have in unwanted births is their ability to "choose" whether or not they want to be a parent. A mother can also give up their child for voluntary adoption. Just like the abortion process, the father's consent is not necessary. Talk about a "Woman's right to choose!"

So let's recap! A woman has the right to choose whether or not to have sex, whether or not to keep a child, whether or not she should be entitled to 50% of your income for 18 years, and whether or not you get to be a regular part of the child's life. Remind me again, are women's rights groups pushing for equality or greater power for themselves? Let me present a scenario.

15

1. A man and woman enter into a relationship. Both agree they don't want children. The woman begins to take birth control pills. The woman decides she wants a child, the man does not agree. The woman stops taking birth control pills without telling her sexual partner, the woman gets pregnant. The man says that he does not want to be a father, = The man is labeled a "deadbeat".

2. A man gets his girlfriend pregnant. The man wants to keep the child; the woman says she does not want to be a mother. Gets an abortion/Gives up child for adoption without telling the father. = Is praised by society for making a tough choice.

Under the 14th amendment of the United States Constitution, "All citizens are guaranteed equal protection under the law." As state and federal laws stand today, women do have the legal protection to choose whether or not they want to become a parent, yet men have absolutely no choice. After all, if a man truly does not want to be a father, isn't it even more damaging to a child's emotional state to chase after a man in the court system who repeatedly denies wanting to be a father? A woman who cannot provide financially for her child gets help, whereas a father who cannot gets incarcerated? Sounds equal huh?

Sarah Weddington, the attorney who presented the *"Roe V Wade"* case to the supreme court in 1973, stated in her testimony that , *"....an unwanted pregnancy can effect a young woman's future, her education, career and create a huge financial burden."* Does she assume that young men who do not want to become fathers and are forced into the family law courts do not have the same fears?

Matt Dubay, who found himself in a similar situation, proposed the idea of a "financial abortion", an idea that is gaining traction in the Swedish parliaments, decided to take his case to the higher courts of Michigan only to find judges citing and reciting cases that proclaim, "The state has a vested interest in child support matters, and declares that children have the right to child support, it is a moot point because the child has already been born and must be provided for. "

Dubay did not take his case to the US Supreme court, but the decision in his case does invite criticism. Is it legal for a married father to not provide financially for his child? Are the "Safe Haven Laws" that protect absentee mothers unconstitutional? Many will say "no" because the government can more than make up for a lack of mothers, after all, in *Article I, sec.8, clause I* of the U.S. Constitution, it states that "..the government has a duty to provide for the general welfare of the people......" unless you are an un-married Father. The government admits it themselves. **Safe-Haven laws** tell us that mothers are indigent and weak, whereas a man who refuses or is unable to be a father is a down right criminal!.Perhaps that is their subtle way of telling us just how important it is that society needs fathers. However, putting them in jail and doing everything you can to impoverish them with legal sanctions is a funny way of expressing this! Let us again explore the philosophical dilemma of feminism.

1. A Woman doesn't want to become a parent, gets an abortion or gives up child for adoption: She is a brave pro-choice woman exercising her right to choose.

2. A man doesn't want to become a parent: Asks to have to his financial and parental obligations absolved: Society says he is a coward, loser, and a deadbeat parent who should be immediately imprisoned.

16

I also find it ironic that "Roe" from "Roe V Wade", Norma McCorvey, later became a staunch supporter of the pro-life movement after her case was decided in her favor. While I am not advocating for abortion or against, what I am asking is that we remain morally and philosophically consistent with the standing laws while considering their rationales. We must ask ourselves, "If such a woman will be affected negatively from a decision, will a man be effected in a similar fashion, and does the law offer them both an equal remedy?"

The answer today is no. Men and women both have methods to help prevent pregnancy. Men have fewer, but they are still present. However, ONLY women have the ability to choose whether or not they want to become parents after conception. Socially, legally, and culturally, men are not allowed to disavow parenthood without serious ridicule and consequence. Women on the other hand are often praised for their efforts of disavowment of parenthood. Although to be fair, women who give/lose custody of their children to fathers are often ridiculed and carry a stigma with them as well; which isn't always warranted.

The Swedish Liberal Youth Party has taken note of this ongoing debate by introducing legislation in 2016 which would allow men to legally absolve their legal responsibilities to a child up until the 18th week of pregnancy, just as a woman has 18 weeks to decide whether or not to abort a child.

Many women's rights advocacy groups were furious upon this hearing of this, stating that women would be furthered burdened by such legislation. Critics argue that allowing men to disavow parenthood would impoverish women and the children involved. Political philosopher, Elizabeth Brake, has often argued in the past that men who accidentally impregnate women should be given more options, and that feminists should oppose policies that coerce a man into fatherhood. Alas, one author from *Feministe.us* , Jill Filipovic, a non practicing lawyer, disagrees. She states, "Aside from adoption, women aren't legally able to absolve parenthood after the child is born." She also states, "These (men's rights) folks aren't asking for equality. They're asking for preferential treatment, above even the state interest in the children."

Her argument quickly falls apart when she says, "Aside from adoption…" In most cases, mothers are able to put their children up for adoption without notifying any would-be father. The opt-out ability is still there.

The logical conclusions are obvious. It comes down to whether or not "pro-life" advocates or "pro-choice" advocates are correct in their thinking. As the law stands today, "pro-choice" advocates have the stage. Thus, if this is the case, then men, under equal protection of the law, have the right to choose parenthood or disavow it. If there is *not* equal protection under the law, and men do not have the right to "choose", then we must revisit whether or not life begins at conception. A fetus begins to develop a heart-beat at 6-weeks post conception. At what magic moment do pro-choicers determine, "ah ha!", "Eureka!", "It is now a human that must be protected!".

At what hour, at what minute, at what event does this special label of "human being" get bestowed upon this "fetus". No pro-choicer can seem to answer this.

Conversely, pro-lifers are highly protective over a fetus, yet, as soon as the child exits the Vagina of an impoverished family, the child and parents are often shamed if they file for welfare benefits, accusing them of being a burden on society. The famous comedian George Carlin once stated,:… "Republicans are pro-life until the child is actually born.-

They don't want to cough up any money for welfare benefits or sign-up to be foster parents. But, they are surprisingly pro-life again once they hit 18, the age they are eligible to be drafted into the military. Or perhaps, these conservatives who enjoy sending these kids to war to die aren't so pro-life after all!"

One thing is certain, with or without a Constitution, any God-fearing person of any spiritual or religious philosophy, believes that a child is not the property of a state but solely to the parents until that child is able to fend for his self in nature. If you have to ask permission to exercise a right then it is not a right but merely a privilege. What next? A parental license that can be suspended? A license itself is simply a right that is transformed and sold into a commodity whereas it can then be revoked, suspended and then sold back to you at a price. Like something out of George Orwell's novel, "1984", author Jack C. Westman proposed this very idea in an article published through PBS in 1996 titled, *"The rationale and Feasibility of Licensing Parents."*

After undergoing personal experiences in the family law courts, countless hours of research and study, interviewing both mothers and fathers, I have come to several conclusions.

Mothers and fathers both play pivotal roles in the development of both boys and girls. Studies reflect disturbing statistics for girls and boys who grow up without a father; with the statistics for children who grow up without a mother are just as disturbing. Boys learn empathy from their mothers. Girls learn self-respect from their fathers; both assume gender roles/identities from watching their male/female counterpart parents. These statements are not cited from a multi-million dollar study, but rather by common sense and observation. As the Chinese would say, men are yang, women are yin, but it takes both to complete the circle that is to make up the continuity of the *Tao. (Nature, God, Harmony.)*

By no means is this report meant to defame or marginalize the struggles of women. In fact, non-custodial women, who make up a minority in family law courts face fewer legal sanctions than non-custodial men, but do face equal if not higher levels of social stigma. A woman who does not have custody of her children is automatically assumed to be a drug addict or deviant. While these circumstances are predominant in cases where women lose custody battles, it is not always so. Libertarian advocates like to assume the philosophy that people should not be seen in groups but rather as individuals. Special privileges or special punishments should not be awarded to anyone because of their race, gender or aspects of a person's biology that is not of their own choosing. I tend to agree with this notion. This is why I cannot endorse any women's or men's rights group, as I see it is important to look at issues from a non-partisan perspective in order to understand and sympathize with any given individual's plight.

This report is our push towards universal human rights. Not for women's rights or men's rights. The final sections of this report will be dedicated towards proposing potential remedies to the aforementioned challenges stated. Recognizing the historical abuses made against both men and women in different quadrants of our social sphere, it is time for us to readjust the scales of liberty and re-establish respect for the 6th,8th,13th,14th amendments of the US constitution, the Universal Declaration of Human Rights, and the unifying principle of a higher power (i.e. creator), that has endowed us all with certain unalienable rights. Among these are life, liberty, and the pursuit of happiness in regards to issues, such as parental alienation, choice, and trafficking/farming of humans.

V.   Proposed Remedies

Problems that ail society can be dissected in debate for hours on end, however, solutions must eventually be proposed. Here I will list several proposals in which I believe will have dramatic positive effects on the family law systems. This report will be submitted to domestic authorities as well as international governing bodies for review. According to my research, the problems and statistics that are referenced to men and women living within the United States are relatable to most other countries who have instituted family law courts as well. Without further interruption, please review the following reformation proposals.

1. **Default 50/50 custody:** This should not even be a proposal but rather a natural conclusion of decent minded human beings. A normal, healthy human being is born with 46 chromosomes. 23 from the mother, 23 from the father. The child does incubate inside of the mother for approximately 9 months, however, if we were to look at the child from the perspective of a joint-partnership creation as in corporate law, the property/creation (i.e. the child), is considered a joint venture of equal responsibly/liability, especially if both parties consented upon its creation. While the mother incubates the fetus, this process would be impossible without the father giving a piece of himself to the incubator (mother). In essence, the initial investment is spent into the mother, whereas the mother agrees to store his property (sperm cell). Where in this transaction can one claim that either party is more entitled to ownership than the other once the incubation process is over?

Under the 14th amendment of the US Constitution, all citizens of the United States are guaranteed equal protection under the law. The gender of a parent does not prove the "fitness" of a parent by default. When paternity is established in a court of law, default 50/50 custody should naturally be the ruling. In fact, custody should not even be discussed unless a parent objects and can bring **strong** evidence that the child has been abused by the other parent, not "likely to be abused", since no party can be and shall be penalized for a crime/action that is yet to be committed. Even new parents who have questionable records should be given the chance to prove themselves as parents. If at a later date, it is shown that the child in question has undergone abuse by either parent, then questions of visitation and custody modifications can be discussed.

To award mothers default custody upon the birth of a child, and then expect a father to potentially spend thousands of dollars in legal fees to prove his fitness as a potential parent, without mandating that the mother to do the same, is discriminatory and veers to the side of misandry. In July of 2016, Missouri passed legislation that encourages default 50/50 custody. While the law itself isn't quite a "mandate", it is a push in the right direction. Among my proposals, this one should be the easiest one to push for and adopt as a world-wide norm.

In Israel, fathers' rights activists staged protests against what they viewed as discriminatory divorce laws and family court policies, made an appeal to the United Nations which resulted in a UN condemnation of Israel for discrimination against divorced fathers. In November of 2014, laws were reformed in Israel that made default joint-custody a legal precedent, however, enforcement of this practice fluctuates.

19

In Hungary, Shared parenting cannot be requested by one parent, it is unregulated. The Family Court must 'place the children' and it must suspend the other parents' rights after divorce/separation. Currently, joint-custody agreements between parents make up less than 1% of all parenting plans.

In Germany, only one parent may apply to the family court for the sole right of custody. The court will agree to such an application if they decide the removal of joint custody and transfer of custody to one parent is in the child's best interests. As of May 2013, non-married Fathers; in order to obtain "Shared Custody" is only possible through marriage or by the mother signing a declaration of shared custody, essentially giving mothers dictatorial powers in custody agreements. Sole custody granted to fathers is not realistic or tangible under the current German family law. The German Supreme Court (Bundesverfassungericht) ruled on July 21st, 2010, that the Family Laws system presiding over custody disputes, violated the German constitution.

Joint custody filings in Germany can be easily defeated when either parent objects. See Constitutional Court decision 1 BvR 738/01 from March 1, 2004, paragraph II. 1. a) The third sentence is translated into English as: "The joint exercise of parental responsibility presupposes a viable social relationship between the parents and requires a minimal level of agreement between them." If one parent refuses to cooperate, the court changes joint custody to sole custody. The law governing the choice of parent receiving sole custody is based on "best interests of the child", (which in my opinion is arbitrary and relies too much on discretion.) The non-cooperation of a parent is not a factor when determining "best interests of the child" and therefore which parent receives sole custody. A parent can refuse to cooperate in order to force a decision in favor of sole custody and then be eligible to win sole custody after refusing to cooperate with the other parent. In essence, mothers who are granted custody and given discretion when and if they disagree with a judge's decision or the father. Statistics prove this.

These are just a few examples of how fathers have been marginalized in the family law courts from around the world. If these issues were isolated, this report would not be warranted for submittal to any international authorities. As you can see, the situation has improved slightly, but the road ahead is still very much in need of attention. Default, 50/50 custody is not only a logical conclusion, but it is the manner in which nature deems fit. Unless there is clear and evident abuse being conducted upon the child in question by one of the parents, there is not a single study published that perpetuates the idea that children gain any advantage by being raised primarily by one parent. In every parenting study published that I have come across, there is an obvious consensus that children gain steep advantages in all areas of social development, when both parents are actively participating in a child's upbringing.

Children who grow up with one of their parents, especially in cases where the child is being actively denied access to a parent who seeks a relationship with his/her offspring, are likely to develop, "Parental Alienation Syndrome", as well as the alienated parent themselves. Parental Alienation Disorder or (PAD) is a condition coined by *Professor William Bernet, Professor of Psychiatry at Vanderbilt University, Nashville,Tn, USA,* and is classified as one of several forms of emotional child abuse. Considering all of these factors, one cannot logically remain an opponent of default 50/50 custody. This is not only a parental rights issue, but also a child's right issue.

A child has the right to have two parents who both wish to participate in his/her life, an issue that has not been addressed, even within the United Nations sponsored, *"Convention on the Rights of the Child"*, instituted in 1989, yet the UN saw it important enough to seek international enforcement of child support collections during the *"Hague Convention on the International Recovery of Child Support and other Forms of Family Maintenance*(i.e.Alimony)". Men who do not pay child support and alimony are considered international criminals, yet the women and/or authorities who play against a man's desire to be in the life of his children are considered legally within their rights to exercise their own free-will and discretion. Quite ironic! Financial gain is always the forefront of any human who holds the axis of power.

2. Reforms to Child Support and Spousal Support.

Just as proposed in Sweden, men should be able to opt out of parenthood just as women are allowed to under current legal norms. From an American perspective, this again is an issue with the 14th amendment. The genitalia of a person should not determine whether or not they are entitled to special protections. Hypothetically speaking, how would custody and support cases, be treated if the two parents in question were a homosexual couple? Who would be considered the mother and who the father? The courts would be forced to look at the facts of the case with disregard to gender.

This rationale is especially relevant in cases where female partners mislead their male counterparts about contraceptive measures. A husband should be able to trust his wife that she is taking contraceptive and has not purposefully or negligently failed to do so and then is rewarded financially for it if a divorce is sought afterwards. In the age of , "No fault divorces", a woman could potentially enter into a marriage with a wealthy man, purposefully mislead her husband about her contraceptive methods, become impregnated, and then file for a 'no fault" divorce (divorce without reason), and then be entitled to a lifetime of alimony payments, whereas if the husband fails to make such payments, he would be incarcerated.

Personally, I would like to see the practice of alimony abolished, for women and male filers. (Yes, some men do collect alimony from women.) The choice to not work or be employed is one that is voluntary, whereas such decisions should not be rewarded because of a divorce. However, if this cannot be achieved, I would like to see alimony limited to 1 year increments. If a spouse has not worked during the tenure of a marriage for the last five years of his/her marriage, he/she could potentially receive a one year "transitional" period of alimony to allow themselves to transition back into single life. The practice of "lifetime alimony", has no logical argument whatsoever. Under the 13th amendment of the US constitution, involuntary service is unlawful.

From a child support perspective, joint custody should become a default process in family law courts with a child support order of $0. If after 12 months from the initial filing in family law courts, if one of the parents can prove that the other parent that the other parent did not have guardianship of the child in question for at least 182 days out of the year, (minus special circumstances like staying with other family members in durations of less than one month, overnight hospital stays, or other events beyond reasonable control), then a child support order can be ordered for a temporary 3 month period whereas the "offending" parents involvement can reevaluated.

In family law courts, it is recognized that the age of 7 is also the "age of reason". The medically recognized period in a child's development when they are cognizant of moral judgments.

The older a child is, their input becomes increasingly relevant. Children who are under the age of 18 should be able to voice their opinions when sanctions are brought against non-custodial parents who are behind on child support payments. If the child expresses that the incarceration of the offending parent would effect him/her negatively, the courts should seek alternative methods of obtaining payment or working out affordable settlement plans and/or parenthood investment programs (to be discussed in my next proposal).

Upon reaching the age of 18 or upon legal emancipation, the child in question should have the right to pardon and/or forgive the non-custodial parent of any arrearage or criminal sanctions brought against his parent. Pundits claims that child support payments are not the custodial-parents' money, but belong to the interest of the child. It is this reason that adult children are legally able to sue their parents for back-child support and in some cases, college tuition fees. The custodial parent is merely considered a "trustee" of the child's money until they reach the age of majority. As explained in Section IV of this report, many adult children have opted to pay child support payments for their parents who fell behind in payments while they were a minor. A practice that is supposed to protect minor children is in some causing them further burdens as adults. If it's truly about the children, then the child's voice should have a major precedent in all matters regarding family law, as a child and as an adult child who has been a party to that system.

The family law courts also need to consider state and national living standards. If a father is only making 20K (gross), and the courts determine that the father is to pay $500 per month in child support, that brings his yearly gross pay to 14K. If he is required to pay for medical insurance and half of daycare fees, his child support expenses could easily reach $700 per month. Once federal tax deductions, Medicare, and his own personal medical insurance deductions are calculated, it is feasible to say that this father (or non-custodial parent), would have less than $10,000 per year to live upon.

With his income being effected in such a way, the idea of obtaining housing, adequately feeding himself, obtaining transportation in a city where public transit is of low-standards, and other basic amenities that most people enjoy, how can he be expected to remain in compliance with the order? Considering that most employers require an applicant to have a mailing address, and with a disposable yearly income that is below $10,000 dollars, the risk of becoming homeless is high. If one finds himself homeless, his employment prospects become low. And if his employment prospects become low, then his chance of incarceration for not being to comply with the child support order becomes high. If he becomes incarcerated, then his chances for gaining suitable employment becomes even lower. The hole just continues to be dug deeper and deeper while the courts sit idle on the sidelines, shaming the father for not being able to keep up.

When considering a child support order, and when considering the best interests of the child, the courts should naturally have an interest in the welfare of the parents as well. (See the general welfare clause in the *US Constitution, Article I, Sec.8, clause I.*) Logically, if the parents are healthy and stable, the child will benefit from a trickling down method. Stronger parents=Stronger children. When one or both of the parents are faced with burdensome court orders, the courts are also punishing the very children that they claim to want to protect as well as putting excessive work on their own administrators. Furthermore, there should be caps on child support and alimony. If a man is making $5,000 per month, and he is ordered to pay out 50% of his income, then that means that the custodial parent will receive $2,500, per month.

That is $30,000 per year(tax free). More than what many Americans make in a single year. If you consider the average housing costs in Tennessee, the lowest rent prices for non-governmental housing in metro Nashville, is about $750 per month. After water and electricity, your monthly rate could be close to $900. In this scenario, the man is expected to pay for the ex-wife's housing expenses, utilities, and then some irrespective of his own living expenses. But who cares if the father ends up homeless right? He shouldn't have subjected himself to a divorce! Everyone knows that unwed fathers are criminals!

Child support orders should also consider "net" incomes, not gross. In some states, such as New York, where there is a state income tax and a federal tax deduction, many workers have as much as 40% of their paychecks garnished by the government even before any child support orders are put in place! Alas, in most jurisdictions, including my home state of Tennessee, it is the "gross" income that is considered. The government does not consider their own confiscations in these matters.

These issues lead me into the next proposal.

3. Giving preference to "Development" rather than "Enforcement" of Sanctions:

Child advocate attorneys are often used in cases where there is abuse or neglect of a child who lives in a single parent home or in the home of married parents. However, they are rarely used when there is a custody dispute between a custodial parent and non-custodial parent whereas private attorneys are often pitted against eachother. The reason being, in the first example, it is the *State VS the parents*, whereas in the second example, it is *parent V parent*.

Again, it is a classic example of how the family law courts are unnecessarily adversarial. One of my biggest complaints is against the Department of Human Services. They are mostly responsible for encouraging and bringing forth custody/support cases on behalf of the "custodial parents" (usually women), to the family law courts. In most of my experiences, these offices are primarily employed by female staff members and zealous case workers who advocate on behalf of the rights of custodial parents and their children. The Department of Human services needs to adopt a "Parental Development Program", or a "Fatherhood Development Program", if they are going to continue to give preference to mothers in custody disputes.

Instead of issuing threats through seizures, intimidating mailing notices, and arrest warrants for non-custodial parents who have not been able to keep up with their child support orders, this system that claims to advocate on the interest of the child, should take interest in both parents, including the non-custodial parent.

If custodial parents (usually mothers), are assigned case workers that aid and guide them on how to apply for welfare benefits, government housing, and educational grants, then why aren't fathers, who are also parents to that child, assigned case worker advocates who will instruct the father on how to better his own living situation?

Instead of incarcerating dead-broke, dead-tired fathers, as opposed to deadbeat fathers (fathers who raised their children for a number of years then decide to abandon their children later on), the system should assist them in order to remain compliant with the order.

It would ease the financial and mental burdens of the mother, the father, the child, the courts, and the prisons. These fathers should be able to access their case worker until the order is completed, altered, or terminated as such that would not require a case worker.

In lieu of incarcerating or suspending a parent's drivers license who is behind on payments, the parent should receive the option to have his payments suspended, deferred and/or reduced in exchange for entering into a special investment program. This program would put fathers in touch with a career/life coach who would help this father obtain training and gain employment that pays atleast the medium national average income of $42,000 per year. In order to qualify for this program, you would have to make under the national average income or your net income would have to be lower than what is feasible to obtain basic housing in your region, even after public assistance. If the father holds onto this job that pays $42,000 or above and is able to stay current with his child support payments, after one year, he could qualify for partial or total arrearage forgiveness to help him stay current. (Pending the child is not undergoing any special circumstances like surgery or chemotherapy that would warrant otherwise.) I do believe that these courts should look at the living situation of the child when considering modifications, reductions, or forgiveness of arrearages as well.

If a father is having a hard time keeping up, yet the child is still being well looked after and fed, (perhaps the mother comes from a wealthy family who is giving her voluntary financial aid), these things should be factored in. If both parents are making equal amounts of money on paper, yet the mother is living in a two-story house and has a recent model car, yet, the father is driving a 15 year old car and is living in low-income housing with fear constant fear of eviction, something is seriously wrong! "We must save the women and children!". This has always been the norm in the age of chivalry, but times have changed, men need help too.

As a man who has had personal experiences as a Bankruptcy specialist, practiced in multi-areas of laws as a paralegal, as a participating defendant, and as a plaintiff in various venues of court, (immigration, criminal, civil, traffic, family)....... This is a scenario that I have scene far too often. Those who are living in poverty, both men and women, are constantly penalized and marginalized for the sake of not being able to "net" enough money to survive, thus, they some peons of the legal system with no ammunition to fight back with. This is especially rampant in traffic and immigration courts, where the poor are lined up to be legally slaughtered in droves. Deportations and suspended drivers licenses, what a racket! (But I digress).

4. Protecting the Sovereignty of Native and Domestic Children from DCS/DHS intrusion

The Indian Welfare Act of 1978 was enacted to do just that! Prevent the arbitrary separation of native children and their parents in cases of family law disputes, foster care, adoption, and removal due to unfit parents. In some ways it has been beneficial while in others, it has been merely a symbolic empty gesture.

While the Indian Welfare Act does place some initial powers back into the hands of Tribal governments, ultimately, the US Federal Government still has the power to supersede any Tribal Law ruling in order to step in and remove a child according to their standards. (Not Tribal Law standards of Fit vs Unit Parents.)

24

Despite a federal law that ties Title IV-E funding to a requirement that CPS/DS seek to place a child with a relative first, many parents allege that this is not being done, and they may be correct according to the Child Welfare Report of 2014. According to the report, only 42.7% of children removed from their homes in Arizona are placed with other family members; Arizona being one state that has a large Indigenous population, a 50% increase over the last five years. When children, especially Native children, are removed from their homes, often times it takes years for the natural parents to regain custody. After such time has passed, they find that their children have become completely unrecognizable.

Allegations of abuse from foster parents, "white washing" of Indigenous children, such as foster parents not allowing them to practice their culture, are also common. Increasing distrust and fear of the Department of Child Services has been mounting. In today's society, children are often taught in public schools to report their parents if they feel abused. Of course, in a child's mind, "abuse" can mean many things. Or, in the case of many allegations, a child makes an innocent comment around another adult about their parents that could be misconstrued, turns into a case that is blown out of proportion. According to the Child Maltreatment report of 2012, 3.2 million children were investigated for claims of abuse by themselves or another adult. 2.5 million of those children were deemed to be "non-victims". The report claims that as a result of deeming those 2.5 million children as "non-victims", 1,640 of them died as a result.

When it comes to DCS, the family law court systems, or any other government agency, the arguments from pundits have always been the same. "They are doing too much!" or "They are not doing enough!"- Yet another reason why alternative private systems of governance and arbitration are becoming more popular among a growing "libertarian" wing in American politics.

The legitimacy or replacement of DCS is a topic that is far beyond the scope of this publication. However, I believe that most of my readers would agree that reforms are in order. Earlier I was speaking of Arizona; good news did recently arise out of state. A bill was introduced that would require a signed warrant from a judge in order for DCS to remove a child from the home of legal guardians. Greg McKay, Director of DCS, reacted by saying, "Whether the bill passes or not, I'll start doing it anyway." If Mr. McKay is being truthful, then this is encouraging news to hear! By giving DCS one more hurdle to jump over, it will potentially slash the number of children being removed from homes and allow more adequate time for parents to remedy any allegations of being "unfit'.

As in cases with custodial parents falling behind in child support payments, the goal of DCS should not be to imprison parents or to take away their children, but to validate claims of abuse/neglect, clarify what constitutes as such (relying on sound evidence), and then seek a remedy to the issue(s). The first remedy relied upon should always be the rehabilitation of sound parenting. Taking away children should be the last resort.

Once children are removed, assisting the parents with correcting the problems that caused the removal with the goal of replacing the child back into the home as quickly as possible, should be the prescription to these allegations. While "removed" children who are placed in the care of non-relative foster homes, DCS should be continuously searching for "next to kin" relatives who are able and willing to take on the child(ren) in question.

In regards to indigenous children, the situation is much bleaker. When you study the statistics, social standards on American Indian Reservations are comparable, if not worse, than some third world nations. The Pine Ridge reservation, home to the famous Lakota Sioux tribe, is well-known because of actor/activist "Russell Means", who raised much awareness for the plight of modern American Indians. Means, who died from cancer complications in 2012, was a staunch support of American Indian sovereignty. In fact, before his death, he was pushing for complete withdrawal from US Federal jurisdictions, proposing the idea that the Pine Ridge Reservations, or as he called them, "Prison of War Camps", become a sovereign nations, completely independent of US customs, rules, and laws.

He even went so far as to say that ,"White people" who have grown tired of tyranny and corruption, can burn their social security cards and come to Pine Ridge to be accepted as Tribesmen. Means was in the process of drawing up plans for funding, public University architectural designs, and the restructuring of Native councils. His proposal would come to be known as, "The Republic of Lakota Proposal". However, after his death, leadership and moral began to drop once more for the Lakota nation.

His idea, called far-fetched by some, had much merit. Technically, the treaties established between the US Federal Government and various Native American Tribes are still quite valid. While the enforceability of such treaties has been ignored, the philosophical claim to it is still very much logical. The "Black Hills Land Claim", being one of the more famous disputes that are still ongoing today between the US Federal Government and the Lakota Sioux Tribe.

Take it from Jacob Dehaven, a wealthy merchant who went bankrupt lending the United States Congress, at the request of George Washington, the equivalent of $141 billion dollars in today's time, worth of gold and supplies, in order to fund his army. Dehaven was never paid back and died with many financial woes. Over the generations, descendants of Dehaven have tried to sue the federal government to reclaim the loan, but all have been unsuccessful. The case is still currently pending with family members who now say, "We don't even want money anymore. We just want Jacob to have recognition, a statue, something to honor him. If not for his sacrifice, the United States would have never become a country because the Revolutionary war would have likely been lost."

Taking these historical precedents in account, the American Indians aren't likely to gain sovereignty from DCS or the federal government anytime soon. However, an act of good faith towards these historically victimized people would be to give them the power of self-determination. Means himself has frequently stated that American Indians have become so dependent upon the Federal government and have so become mentally enslaved, that they have forgotten how to run their own affairs. Suicide rates, alcoholism, and poverty rates on reservations are among some of the highest in the world. This is quite Shocking when you consider that these reservations are located within the jurisdiction of the United States of America; one of the most powerful and wealthiest nations on Earth.

Two simple reforms to the widespread epidemic of American Indian Children being ransacked from their villages would be to help transition full responsibility over family affairs to the Tribal governments. The US government can continue to preside over other legal issues regarding Native American sovereignty; however, the family unit is a sacred thing to humanity, one to which should belong solely to the people themselves, especially to American Indians, who have been lied to during

26

the creation of every US-Native Treaty presented to them. The least that can be given to them is full power over the affairs of their children. Children are the life-blood to any race, culture, clan, or tribe. When the children of a society are born into chaos, they bring forth a generation of grandchildren that are raised by children who were also born into said chaos. We need to shift momentum back towards self-governance, individual responsibility, freedom of choice, and a return to universal respect of life, liberty, and the pursuit of happiness, all of which are endowed by our creator, not by our governments.

The second reform, which would apply to all DCS cases, both tribal and domestic, would be the federal mandate of removal warrants signed at the discretion of a judge.

A judge should be given a period of time to look over the facts of the case and to use **factual discretion** to disagree with DCS's request to remove and call for a secondary hearing to discuss removal. Many Americans complain about the slow process of our legal system, however, occasionally, that slow process works to our advantage. When litigation or legal processes move at a slower rate, it can deter people from taking unnecessary legal actions. As in the case of restraining order dockets, which are normally inflated and quick moving, it is the ease of application that sometimes invites the presumption of abuse. In the case of DCS, having the ability to involuntarily remove a child from their parents, the process should be slow and painful for the government, not for the parent, unless there is an extreme circumstance where it is clear and evident that a child is in imminent danger. In such cases, a Judge could swiftly sign and agree on removal.

5. Convention on the Elimination of all Forms of Gender Discrimination

CEDAW (Convention on the Elimination of all Forms of Discrimination against Women), was adopted in 1970. Since then, domestic violence, rape, sexual trafficking, and other related issues that had been historically attributed to female victims, has finally received international recognition. As the author of this text, I myself agree that the female gender has experienced marginalization within our social construct. Alas, being born into the male gender also presents unique challenges and opportunities to be discriminated against; which has not received international recognition. I propose that the issues presented within this document be discussed, whereas every four years, member states will agree to have their domestic policies reviewed in terms of gender equality and equal protection under the law. Some have proposed the idea of a (CEDAM) (Convention for Men), however, I believe that such terminology further ignites the gender war. I propose that the CEDAW treaty be dropped and replaced with a gender neutral tone (Convention on the Elimination of all Forms of Gender Discrimination) that addresses discrimination against both sexes, whereas there will be no special privileges or punishments for anyone based upon their genitalia. I will personally volunteer myself to speak during such a convention in order to address these matters.

VI.   General/Personal Charges and Complaints

On October 17th, 2016, I filed a motion to remove jurisdiction from the Davidson County, Nashville,Tn, USA, family law courts into a U.S. District Federal Jurisdiction in order to address civil rights violations and Constitutional questions, all of which are valid reasons to move a State case into a Federal Venue.

27

The case#3:16-cv-02729, was filed and recorded for the public record, via "pro se". PACER can verify the documents that were sent whereas I addressed most of the issues raised within this publication. Case studies on the ramifications of parental alienation and the lack of equal protection under the law, via the 14th Amendment of the Constitution, being the paramount arguments. The State of Tennessee, as well as every other State within the United States, and the United States Federal Government itself, has consistently ruled against the idea that men have equal protection under the law when it comes to custody and support orders. Currently, there is not a single state within the United States that recognizes default joint custody upon neither birth nor men having the ability to choose or absolve parenthood. The famous Michigan case of *"Matt Dubay vs Lauren Wells- UNITED STATES COURT OF APPEALS FOR THE SIXTH CIRCUIT. 6 Nov. 2007."* , was well publicized and touted as the "Roe V Wade for Men", but was struck down. Dozens of other cases have surfaced to no avail. Governments around the world, especially in the United States, appear to have absolutely no interest in advancing the plight of would be fathers.

My federal case was dismissed on November 17th and remanded back to the Juvenile court of Davidson county, Tn, for supposed lack of Jurisdiction. On or around February 13th of 2017, my passport and federal income tax refunds were administratively suspended during my appeal. The state of Tennessee in conjunction with DHS, cited that I owed $7,000 during the months I was not aware of my parentage. I was also made aware that I would be fully responsible for any and all medical expenses pertaining to the child until he reached the age of 18, because I was the "non-custodial" parent. If I could not afford medical insurance for the child, they informed me that I would be charged with "medical arrears." Essentially, such a determination has turned me into a land-locked prisoner, who isn't allowed to leave his country, choose a new nationality, travel, or be financially independent, for the crime of being a father. Additionally, during this entire process, I was never advised or encouraged on how to assert my supposed rights to be involved with the child, yet I was consistently threatened with the repercussions of not being able to meet their financial obligations unlawfully placed against me. I have only seen the child on two major occasions.

To further litigate these matters domestically appears fruitless. This is why I am reaching out to the international community and its relevant governing bodies to assist me in these matters. I seek reformations in the law that gives both genders default custody upon birth, the ability for both genders to choose or absolve parenthood up until the 1st trimester, reforms in child support/alimony and for the Department of Human Services to create public "fatherhood advocate" case workers/attorneys to assist men in such cases as women are currently being treated and represented in the family law courts. I also ask that the suspension of Passports in regards to arrearages be overturned unless there is clear criminal intent to commit an international crime. **Article 13 of the Universal Declaration of Human Rights** asserts that: "a citizen of a state in which that citizen is present has the liberty to travel, reside in, and/or work in any part of the state where one pleases within the limits of respect for the liberty and rights of others" and that "…a citizen also has the right to leave any country, including his or her own, and to return to his or her country at any time."

I desire my day in a neutral international court setting to address the United States of America in regards to these matters as well as the UN Human Rights Council to discuss a possible gender neutrality treaty.

28

I later discovered further evidence that the state and federal governments of the United States are involved in a "quasi" human trafficking scheme through the federal law, **Title IV, section D of the Social Security Act- Child Support.** According to the law, when the state collects a certain amount of child support payments from non-custodial parents, the federal government matches those funds in the form of a grant to be given to the collecting states on a yearly basis. Many lawmakers tout Title IV section D as an "incentive" program for states to enforce child support orders and to reduce welfare expenditures, however, the incentive appears to be, "Collect child support through any means necessary so that we may receive our "incentive" bonus from the federal government!". By essentially putting a bounty on a child's life, the court no longer has an incentive to protect the life and emotional well-being of children and "non-custodial" parents, but rather the incentive is to generate revenue at the cost of human life and emotional well-being of the family unit as a whole. The incentive to grant joint-custody to both parents with no order of child support, (which should be the standard except for in special circumstances), is completely removed by way of Title IV section D of the Social Security Act.

As I have explained throughout the course of this manifesto, the family law courts and the way they are currently operating contribute to homelessness, increased bankruptcy filings, teen pregnancy, suicide, and nearly every social ill that we can imagine. As human nature has shown throughout the history of economic systems, when the incentive of obtaining funds is embedded with the legal authority to imprison a man for having a lack of funds, state sponsored human trafficking, dictatorships, slavery, and other forms of citizen abuse become the norm. Although these actions are disguised through formal court proceedings, the negative effects and emotional trauma that such a system has bred can only be identified by those who have been on the receiving end of such a decree or by those empathetic enough to independently research the matter.

Let us recap the courts money making revenue scheme: 1. Man pays child support 2. Title IV rewards the state. 3. Man doesn't pay child support 4. Man goes to jail. 5. Prisons make money through contracts with the state. 6. Lawyers & Judges are paid and have their jobs justified regardless of the outcome.

My readers should ask themselves this. Why is there a child-support enforcement agency that punishes non-payers, yet there is no "Child Visitation Enforcement Agency", that monitors and punishes custodial parents who alienate children from the non-custodial parents? Because generating revenue is a primary concern, whereas making sure that children and non-custodial parents are treated with dignity and compassion is of secondary concern. In fact, in many cases, the state will readily agree to take a child into their custody so that they may receive child support and Title IV payments from the Federal Government. They have created an ingenious way to use the plight of women and children to ruthlessly extract money from would-be fathers or divorced dads.

The scheme is despicable, yet it is also ingenious on their part. If I were devoid of any emotional empathy, I would implement a similar system so that I too may become a financial mogul. At the very least, Title IV section D should be removed from the Federal code completely in order to remove such bias and immoral incentives to destroy families in order to gain a profit instead of working together to strengthen them.

29

VII. Conclusion

The purpose of this publication is not meant to discredit or downplay the struggles of any gender, race, nationality, or creed. I personally recognize that every race, gender, and governmental nation has faced challenges and unfair treatment, both internally and externally. With enough research, anyone can find biased facts that will support his/her argument.

In the information age, it isn't very difficult to find a study or statistic that supports one's personal narrative or "sales pitch". Yet it isn't always about the research that is done, but the experiences that are lived. As I write this publication, I reflect back upon my vast experiences as a political activist, legal analyst, and someone who has lived with and been involved in romantic and business relationships with people that do not share my nationality or racial make-up.

I have purposefully lived out my life in this manner. Whether I was spending time with my Cambodian friends in a Buddhist temple, or mingling with my predominantly Muslim co-workers during my tenure at *Dell Computers*. Whether I was protesting with the anti-war liberals, the anti-tax conservatives, or the pro-free market libertarians, I can honestly say to anyone during any debate, regardless of the topic at hand, **"You make a fair point".** It's a powerful phrase that allows one to place his consciousness into another's. It's called "empathy".

Considering these experiences and the plethora of different views that have been introduced to me throughout my 30 years walking upon this Earth, as a child who grew up in divorce, and as one who experienced the family law courts as an adult participator, I firmly believe that my assessments are accurate and valid. The merits of my arguments are sound, unbias and deserve consideration. I plan to submit this publication to local, federal, and international governing bodies as well as private organizations.

My goal is to create reforms in legislation and to create an international dialogue in regards to the aforementioned statements made throughout this publication. I am more than willing and able to speak on behalf of these issues personally. On behalf of **Nalini-Global**, I, Randell Stroud, hope to be invited to any relevant United Nations conferences as a non-member observer, so that I may have the authority to speak on a larger platform.

I pray that this publication will be taken in good faith that my intentions are to promote equality and universal human rights. I do not advocate on behalf of increasing the rights of any particular group of people, as I am vehemently against collectivism. I do not consider myself a women's or Men's rights activist, but as a human rights activist.

My prior activism record includes reforms in traffic court, Council on Foreign Relation's attitudes towards Foreign Policy & Diplomacy, repealment of legislation that threatens civil liberties such as the National Defense Authorization Act's "indefinite detention clause", the Patriot Act, and many others. In fact, my activism blossomed in 2010 when I lead a joint effort with Nashville's at the time District Attorney, Torry Johnson, who aided me in stripping Davidson county clerk, John Arriola, of his position for embezzling money while officiating public wedding ceremonies.

So you see, when private individuals work in conjunction with governmental powers in a logical fashion where open dialogue and mutual respect become the cornerstones of debate, wonderful things happen!

Let us not forget the international charter of the ancient "Magna Carta", which spearheaded a push for international recognition of universal human rights.

Let us not forget that the United States Constitution was influenced by the six tribal nations of the north and their laws found in the Iroquois Confederation. The struggle to fight for a balance between freedom, security and liberty are challenging.

Let us not forget the wise words of Benjamin Franklin. "Those who would give up essential liberty, to purchase a little temporary safety, deserve neither liberty nor safety." Or as my uncle Shane would say, who spent a large portion of his life behind bars, "I would rather struggle in freedom than to have everything handed to me in prison. I didn't have to cook my meals in prison, but I also didn't have a say in what I ate. I didn't have to make my bed, but I couldn't choose what kind of bed I slept in. I didn't have to pay rent for my room, but I couldn't choose my which room. I didn't have to look for a roommate, one was chosen for me. That's not living, even if it is easier." He's been out of prison for nearly three years now working an honest job in construction and doesn't plan to ever go back. Earning a living is hard, but giving over your life to a system of control is even harder.

Please accept my invitation to consult with me on these matters and/or to attend any relevant hearings, conventions, or events where my voice of reason may be of benefit to you.

May God bless every race, gender, and nation of humans residing upon this world we call home, planet Earth.

Sincerely,

Randell Stroud

Co-Founder of Nalini-Global

Naliniglobal.wordpress.com

Naliniglobal@yahoo.com

Major Sources:

US Census

Department of Justice CNN

Federal Bureau of Investigation

United Nations General Comments, Declarations

Department of Labor and WorkForce Development

Council on Foreign Relations

CPSIA information can be obtained
at www.ICGtesting.com
Printed in the USA
BVOW04s1402161117
500586BV00005BA/387/P

9 781387 232017